Of this edition of

JOHN EVANS—AN APPRECIATION

a limited number of copies has been

printed. This is number _____

printed especially for

_____

JOHN EVANS

1814 - 1897

AN APPRECIATION

by

WALTER DILL SCOTT
President of Northwestern University

Privately Printed

By Courtesy of Lester J. Norris

1939

Evanston, Illinois

JOHN EVANS

1814-1897

Foreword

The subject of this brief biographical sketch is Dr. John Evans, for whom the City of Evanston, Illinois, was named. He has had a greater influence in the life of the City of Evanston and of Northwestern University, and has done more to create our traditions and to determine the line of our development, than any other individual. The purpose of this biography is to present him as a physician, as a railroad builder, as a city builder, as an educator, as a religious leader, and as a political leader.

Data for this sketch have been secured from *The Life of John Evans* by Edgar Carlisle McMechen, from records and histories of Northwestern University, from the files of newspapers, from medical journals, from histories of Colorado, and from biographical dictionaries and encyclopaedias. Excerpts from *The Life of John Evans* appear without acknowledgment.

CHAPTER I.

John Evans, Physician

THE FATHER of John Evans was a merchant in Waynesville, a small town in Ohio. He desired that his son should succeed him in the store, but early in life John became convinced that his greatest usefulness could be attained only in the medical profession. In this ambition he was opposed by his mother as well as by his father, and it was only after a bitter struggle that he brought himself to go contrary to the advice of his parents and to heed the call of duty as he saw it. The following is an extract from a letter which John wrote to his cousin, Benjamin, and which describes his mental processes in reaching this conclusion:

> I intend to encounter as few difficulties as possible, but when one presents I will move it aside and still pursue that course which I now lay down to that glorious distinction which shall be his who most advances the amelioration of his fellow beings . . . . . Only to think of following a trade for no other purpose than my own pecuniary advantage! I am persuaded there was something more than this meant when I was made. I have long been of this notion, and for me, by irresolution, to thwart the design of my creation would be more wicked than a refusal to knuckle to any particular mode of getting along in the world, or any particular creed of faith. It is the imperative voice of the Almighty that we

shall do all the good we can, and my doctrine is, he is the best man who comes nearest fulfilling the mandate.

John had no money and was too proud, under the circumstances, to ask his father to pay for a course of medical instruction. Two practicing physicians in Waynesville, however, agreed with the stand John had taken and approved his attitude in not asking his father for money. They therefore most generously provided the cash to meet the expenses of his professional training at Lynn Medical College in Cincinnati. There he studied under such distinguished teachers as Samuel D. Gross, soon to become the most eminent surgical leader in America, and Daniel Drake, who was the outstanding medical leader of the Middle West. As he asserted in a letter dated November 13, 1837, and directed to Hannah Canby, who later became Mrs. John Evans, John was a most industrious and conscientious student:

> If you will not attribute it to vanity I will say I think I am about as devoted a student as we have in the college—my waking hours are almost wholly occupied in study and I very frequently dream over whole demonstrations after hearing them in the day —So you see I think pretty well of my industry whatever others may say of it.

When John returned with his diploma, his father relented and presented him with a pony, a saddle, and ten dollars. With these assets, he rode from his home in Ohio and after inspecting various fields of labor finally reached the village of Attica, Indiana, where he began the practice of medicine. In this obscure rural center he intended to specialize in obstetrics, but found himself called to other specializations too. The blind, the deaf, and the insane in Attica, as everywhere, were inadequately and unintelligently cared for; Dr. Evans turned to them, and it was in connection with these unfortunates that he made his first conspicuous contributions to medicine. In 1844 he cooperated with Henry Ward Beecher and Bishop Matthew Simpson in inducing the State of Indiana to build and to administer its first home and its first school for deaf mutes. He published articles stressing the necessity for more adequate care of the insane and was invited to address a joint session of the Legislature on this subject. Dr. Evans convinced the Legislature of the necessity of prompt action in the erection of an adequate insane asylum. As a result he was asked to move to Indianapolis, and to become a member of the Board which planned and supervised the construction of the Indiana Lunatic Asylum.

At this same time the fame of Dr. Evans had spread to Chicago, and he was invited to become a member of the faculty of Rush Medical College, the only medical school in that city. At the early age of thirty-four he was called upon to decide whether he would remain in Attica, where he had built up a desirable practice, move to Indianapolis and engage in medical administration, or move to Chicago and be-come a professor of obstetrics. Dr. Evans promptly decided to leave his practice in Attica, but could not make up his mind between the opportunities offered at Indianapolis and at Chicago. Accordingly, he agreed to accept the call to teach in Chicago during the winter terms, but to move to Indianapolis and accept the responsibility of planning and equipping the insane asylum and of seeing medical service in-augurated.

By 1848 Dr. Evans regarded his work in Indian-apolis as accomplished, and accordingly moved to Chicago intending to teach in the medical school and to engage in the practice of medicine. But his interests had so widened that many of his energies were spent on projects outside his regular class room teaching and his private medical practice.

Immediately upon entering the practice of medicine Dr. Evans had begun to write for publi-cation. He refers to this in a short biographical sketch:

> When I settled at Attica, Indiana, practicing medicine, I commenced publishing articles in rela-tion to founding institutions for taking care of the insane, who were then kept in poor houses and jails throughout the state.

In 1844 the faculty of Rush Medical College began the publication of the *Illinois Medical and Surgical Journal*. Dr. Evans sent several articles for publication in that journal, one of which was the address delivered before the Legislature of Indiana convened in joint session, entitled, "Insanity and the Establishment of a Lunatic Asylum." The simple logic of that address is well illustrated by a single quotation:

> There is no question of whether we will take care of our lunatic paupers or not, or whether a tax shall be laid for that purpose, for we cannot avoid either, as the counties must provide for them at the expense of the public, if the State does not. And how it is attended to by the counties we have already seen. The only question is, will we adhere to the present yet *miserable* plan, or will we adopt the one dictated by the strongest consideration of economy, and the purest principles of humanity.

Soon after Dr. Evans became a member of the faculty of Rush the title of their journal was changed to the *Illinois and Indiana Medical and Surgical Journal*. Dr. Evans became a member of the editorial board, and the journal was published simultaneously at Chicago and at Indianapolis. In a few years the title was changed to the *Northwestern Medical and Surgical Journal*. For the year 1852 Dr. Evans served alone as editor, but because of the press of other duties was compelled at the end of the year to resign from that position.

In connection with his medical practice, teaching, and writing, Dr. Evans felt the need of a hospital in Chicago. Accordingly he and a few of his associates obtained in 1847 a charter for the Illinois

General Hospital of the Lakes. Dr. Evans and two judges were named as trustees. The next year he met Dr. N. S. Davis in New York and cooperated with Dr. Brainard in inducing him to come to Chicago. Dr. Davis was most helpful in establishing this hospital. At the time of the opening of the hospital there appeared in the *Northwestern Medical and Surgical Journal* an article, presumably written by Dr. Evans, which contained the following paragraph:

> Thus has been commenced an institution which, we trust, with the smiles of an over-ruling Providence, is destined to a long career of usefulness in relieving sickness, pain and sorrow, and which will be a monument to the memory of those who contribute to its endowment and support, more honorable than the laurels of the conqueror.

In Chicago at that time there was a shortage of adequately trained nurses, and an arrangement was made with the resident Catholic Bishop to have the Sisters of Mercy take over the nursing. Later the hospital was renamed Mercy Hospital.

Early in the year 1850 Dr. Evans and a few others began to hold medical meetings at each other's houses and offices. The object was to read papers and discuss cases of common interest. As early as April 5, 1850, the name "Chicago Medical Society" was adopted by them. This same group organized what were called Pathological Sociables. These were continued until after the Chicago fire of 1871. The formal organization changed its name to "Cook County Medical Society" in 1852 but reverted to its original name of "Chicago Medical Society" in 1858. Dr. Evans was thus one of the founders of the Chicago Medical Society. He was also one of the founders of the Illinois Medical Society, which was organized June 3, 1853, at Peoria. He is accredited also with a part in organizing the American Medical Society.

In connection with his professional practice and with his medical teaching, Dr. Evans invented several surgical instruments of great importance, some of which are still used in their original designs. His Obstetrical Extractor is the best known of his instruments.

Some of the social ideals of Dr. Evans brought about radical changes in medical education. According to McMechen, Dr. Evans was a pioneer in the medical education of negroes and of women:

> While a member of the faculty at Rush the first colored medical student in America, a Dr. Peck, was graduated with a degree. The latter found it necessary to move into Canada to secure practice. The first woman admitted to a medical school in this country, Miss Emily Blackwell, who afterward distinguished herself, also was graduated from the College during this period.

In December, 1848, a disastrous plague of Asiatic cholera began to spread into all parts of the United States. Dr. Evans became tremendously interested and carried on elaborate studies of this epidemic. In September, 1849, he published in the *Northwestern Medical and Surgical Journal* his "Observations." The following excerpt from these "Observations" is interesting:

> Cholera is subject to no boundaries except those that prevent human intercourse. When carefully observed, it (cholera) is found uniformly to spread along the lines of intercommunication and travel but never faster than their regular course. It follows shipping routes and lines of railway. It is of a communicable or portable nature.

This theory propounded by Dr. Evans was scouted and attacked by many of the leading physicians of America. Nevertheless, he felt sure of the validity of his conclusion and published his "Observations" in pamphlet form for general distribution. The opposition of the medical profession was so great that no national quarantine laws were possible at that time. However, the process of education was continued, and in 1866 Dr. Evans memorialized Congress for the establishment of a national quarantine law. In this memorial he reprinted the "Observations" from the *Journal* of 1849. A national quarantine law was passed, and experts of that period gave credit to Dr. Evans for this national advance in protection not only against Asiatic cholera but against other communicable diseases. This accomplishment might be thought of as the crowning work of the medical career of Dr. Evans.

CHAPTER II.

John Evans, Railroad Builder

FOR JOHN EVANS as a boy and as a young man travel was by stagecoach or saddle horse; freight was by flat boat, ox cart, or wagons drawn by oxen, mules, or horses. As a pupil living in southwestern Ohio he traveled by stagecoach to and from the boarding school in Philadelphia. As a prospective physician he traveled by saddle horse into the villages of Ohio, Indiana, and Illinois in search of a place to practice. In 1841 money had been driven out of the western states by almost unrestricted bank issues, and at that time Dr. Evans, starting his career at Attica, received his pay in corn, potatoes, and other farm products. Thus, as a young physician there Dr. Evans was forced to procure a flat boat to carry his produce down the Wabash, the Ohio, and the Mississippi rivers to the market in New Orleans, where he could sell his grain and vegetables and purchase the necessary drugs. A few years later Chicago developed as a market for farm products and for drugs, and paid for them with negotiable money. Then Dr. Evans brought his produce to Chicago in a wagon drawn by oxen, and returned to Attica with the drugs in the same conveyance. As a resident of Indianapolis and a member of the medical faculty in Chicago, he "commuted" by stagecoach. As the war governor of Colorado he made the trip from Chicago to Denver in thirteen days by the stagecoach; and for transporting army supplies he depended much on trucks drawn by oxen or mules. In all the instances cited he used only those methods of travel and of transportation that had been available to his ancestors for a century or more.

John Evans had a background of experience that enabled him to appreciate the significance of the steam engine and the railroad. Jay Gould, a contemporary of John Evans, interpreted the steam engine and the railroad as an opportunity to amass great personal profit. John Evans interpreted the steam engine as in reality a public utility. Jay Gould manipulated railroad stock for personal pecuniary reward. John Evans built and managed railroads as a community and as a national convenience and necessity.

In the early fifties three independent but cooperating corporations constructed the first railroad from Pittsburgh to Chicago. The eastern section was constructed by the Pennsylvania and Ohio, the central section by the Ohio and Indiana, and the western section by the Fort Wayne and Chicago. This western section, the Fort Wayne and Chicago, was further subdivided into two parts. One part extended from Fort Wayne to the Indiana state line, and the other part extended from the state line to Chicago and included the terminus with railroad yards and a depot. Dr. Evans was a director of the Fort Wayne and Chicago and had charge of the management and construction of the work west of the Indiana state line. He procured the right of way through Illinois to Chicago, the right of way through the streets of Chicago, and the site for the depot and yard in the City. He purchased for the depot and yard forty acres for $35,000. The following year he sold one-half of this terminal site for $140,000 to the Burlington and Quincy. Steam transportation was then in its infancy, for it was only twenty-two years after construction had been started on the first passenger railroad in the United States, the Baltimore and Ohio. Investors were skeptical of railroads as safe depositories for their money, and it was an extremely laborious task to finance them. All three companies were involved in financial difficulties from their inception, but were finally consolidated and given the general name, Pittsburgh, Fort Wayne and Chicago. Later the system was leased to the Pennsylvania for ninety-nine years. The financing in this instance was recognized as among the ablest accomplished in the early railroad history of the country, and Dr. Evans, as representative of the western branch, deserves some of the credit.

In 1859 Dr. Evans and some of his associates

in Chicago and Evanston reached the conclusion that a railroad to the Pacific Ocean would certainly be constructed in the next few years, and that a great city would probably arise at the point where this railroad crossed the Missouri River. He became convinced that the best place for such a crossing and the best place for such a city was at the point of juncture of the Platte and Missouri Rivers. He foresaw also that a ferry across the river and a rapidly developing community would greatly increase the chances that any contemplated railroad across the plains would select a right of way through that point. Accordingly, he secured a large tract of land at the confluence of the Platte and Missouri Rivers, and laid out a prospective city. A steam ferry system was installed, and the erection of a hotel and numerous other buildings was begun or anticipated. The town was called Oreopolis and in a few weeks became a boom town. However, the plans to construct a transcontinental railroad were unfulfilled, and only the steam ferry became a reality so far as transportation was concerned, and the program was ultimately abandoned.

Dr. Evans' next venture in railroading concerned Evanston. As soon as he became interested in Evanston as a city of homes he recognized the desirability of rapid transportation to and from Chicago. Together with a few friends he organized in 1861 the Chicago and Evanston Railroad, and secured the right of way and sites for stations and yards. The right of way was secured not along the lake front but as far west as convenience would permit. An interesting feature of the plan was the proposal to employ combination steam carriages to carry passengers from Evanston to Chicago's city limits, attach horses to the front of the locomotive there, and thus draw the train into the heart of the business district. It was estimated that a speed of thirty miles an hour could be maintained to the city limits, and six miles an hour made by horse power. The substitution of horses was intended to meet objection from Chicago residents to entrance of a steam locomotive into the business district, an obstacle that was considered certain to arise. After Chicago had become more accustomed to the sight of a locomotive within its city limits, the plan was to discard the horses and come in on steam power. Before the project could be completed the road was purchased by the Chicago, Milwaukee, and St. Paul Railroad Company. Today this right of way is used jointly by the Chicago, Milwaukee, St. Paul and Pacific Railroad Company, the Chicago, North Shore and Milwaukee Railroad Company, and the Chicago Rapid Transit Company.

In 1862 Dr. Evans was appointed by President Lincoln as Territorial Governor of Colorado. There were at that time about twenty-five firms carrying passengers and freight across the great plains. These companies employed a personnel of approximately 15,000 men, and utilized 5,000 wagons, 7,000 mules and horses, and 28,000 oxen. Governor Evans moved his home to Denver and became active in an attempt to secure better transportation facilities there. However, by 1867 the indications were that no transcontinental railroad would pass through Denver, and that it would in a few years change from a prosperous city to a deserted village. In desperation the citizens organized a Board of Trade to promote Denver's railroad interest. This organization promptly projected the Denver Pacific Railroad and Telegraph Company. Governor Evans was first made one of the directors and later the president. The first great task was to secure favorable contracts of cooperation with the Union Pacific and the Kansas Pacific, and then to secure generous land grants from the federal government for the right of way and for the bordering salable land. These preliminary contracts with the railroads and with the federal government were concluded at Washington in March, 1869. The good news reached Denver before Governor Evans could return from Washington by stagecoach. He reached Denver at night and found the city ablaze with lights and bonfires in his honor. A committee of the citizens met him and escorted him to the Board of Trade rooms, where he was presented with an engrossed resolution of gratitude for his services in saving the city.

Great difficulties were encountered in the completion of the railroad. The Board of Trade and the County Commissioners offered Governor Evans $2,500,000 of the road's first mortgage bonds, a substantial stock interest, and other considerations, to take over the contract for completing it. Under urging he consented, and made such rapid progress that by December 16, 1869, trains began to run over one-half the road, and the entire project was assured. Thereupon the citizens in their delight celebrated by naming the great mountain to the west Mt. Evans. This spontaneous action was officially confirmed years later by the Colorado Legislature, which also gave the name of Evans to the projected city that marked the halfway point between Cheyenne and Denver. When finally all the debt and all the expenses connected with the construction of the railroad were paid, Governor Evans had a favorable balance of $500,000. This entire sum he donated to the county of which Denver was the county seat.

The success attained by Governor Evans in completing the Denver Pacific was merely the beginning of his efforts to make Denver a great railroad center. In 1887 success again crowned one of his many railroading achievements, and further honors were bestowed upon him by the Denver Chamber of Commerce. The following is an extract from the engrossed resolution presented to him:

> Resolved, That by the success that has finally crowned the efforts of our esteemed friend and fellow-citizen, Governor John Evans, in providing the means to build the Denver, Texas & Gulf Railroad— a short line to the sea—he has completed a great series of iron roads to Denver, including the Denver Pacific, the Kansas Pacific, the Boulder Valley, and the South Park, mainly through his own efforts, and which have made this city the commercial metropolis of the Rocky Mountain country . . . .

These statements concerning John Evans as a railroad builder are not intended to be in any sense complete. No mention is made, for instance, of his participation in 1890 in the Union Pacific, and in 1894 in the Denver, Sioux City, Lake Superior & Chicago railroads. Since the tunnel now known as the Moffet Tunnel was completed after the death of Governor Evans no mention is made of his long and unsuccessful efforts to build a direct railroad from Denver to the Pacific by digging through the Rocky Mountains. In some of his railroad ventures Governor Evans was most fortunate and in some he lost financially, but his primary objective was to advance the community.

CHAPTER III.

John Evans, City Builder

JOHN EVANS may appropriately be called a city builder because of his constructive contributions to each of six municipalities — Attica, Indianapolis, Chicago, Evanston, Oreopolis, and Denver. To each of these he supplied present needs or provided factors essential for future development. He worked on the theory that cities could be successfully built only by making them into communities to which a superior type of people would be pleased to migrate, and in which they would desire to remain permanently.

Dr. Evans began his practice of medicine in Attica, Indiana, and remained there six years (1839-45). The first few years he was busily occupied in establishing himself in his profession and in becoming acquainted in the community. During these preliminary years he came to realize that Attica, located in a rich agricultural district and on the Wabash River, had great possibilities as a residential community and as a commercial center, but lacked the physical facilities for such developments. Accordingly, he erected in Attica, besides a good residence for himself, the Evans block, a convenient and commodious trading center. Attica lacked any organization, or group of citizens interested in promoting the public welfare of the community. Accordingly, he assembled a group of five progressive citizens, together with their wives, to promote the welfare of Attica. The first project thus sponsored was the care of those mentally and physically handicapped. The activities of this group spread the reputation of Attica throughout the state and even into adjoining states.

Dr. Evans was a resident of Indianapolis for but a part of each of three years (1845-48). His primary activity there was to serve first as one of the three members of the Board of Commissioners for the proposed Hospital for the Insane, and then as the superintendent of this hospital. The hospital was erected on a beautiful tract of land containing 160 acres and located two miles from the center of the city. The site, the architecture of the building, and the care of the patients were so superior that the hospital became a model that had a wholesome influence on the treatment of all classes of unfortunates, locally and nationally.

Attica and Indianapolis were but minor training grounds for the major tasks in city building undertaken by Dr. Evans during the fourteen years (1848-62) which he spent in Chicago. Chicago was young then. Railroad facilities were inadequate; and in the preceding chapter facts were presented to indicate how Dr. Evans contributed in making Chicago a great railroad center.

There was a dearth of adequate office buildings; and in 1851 Dr. Evans secured a twenty-year lease on four lots on the corner of Clark and Randolph streets, on which he built the Evans block. Space in this building was in great demand, and was rented to such tenants as the Chicago Post Office, the Chicago Tribune for an editorial room, and to many of the better professional men. On this building Dr. Evans netted annually $5,000 until the expiration of the lease in 1871.

While serving as alderman Dr. Evans recommended to the City Council that the level of all streets and sidewalks in the lower central parts of Chicago be elevated—in many instances several feet. His recommendation was bitterly opposed, as it would require owners of vacant lots to fill in the land up to the new street level, and it would require the owners of buildings to jack up their buildings to the higher level. After the presentation of the need by Alderman John Evans the City Council approved the recommendation. This was the first lake shore development project of Chicago, and the beginning of the movement to provide for Chicago adequate drainage and a firm foundation. At that time this improvement was spoken of as Chicago's lifting herself out of the mud by her boot straps. This establishing of street grades is an illustration of the work accomplished by Alderman Evans as a member of the Committees on Public Grounds, on Wharves, and on Wharving Privileges. In these projects he helped to build the City from the bottom up.

Dr. Evans took great pride in his success in beautifying the City. In 1894 he prepared an address for delivery in Denver in which he recited some of his achievements in Chicago. The following quotation is illuminating:

> I have had experience that may be useful to some if I relate it—in the inauguration of the system of parks in Chicago. I was then a large landholder, and an active supporter of the movement. We first got a park commission appointed by law, with ample power to purchase land, and where owners would not sell, they had power to condemn and take it. They first provided the land, and through all these twenty-five years since, have been improving it. I was a member of the city council and voted for it when we purchased the first park in Chicago. It is called Union Square. In the extension of the grand system afterward I sold the city the land for part of Blue Island Boulevard.

While Dr. Evans was a citizen of Chicago he did much to make it healthful. In raising the elevation of the land throughout the principal part of the City, he taught the citizens to undertake the almost impossible when the welfare of the City was at stake. It was not strange, therefore, that, when it was proposed in the interest of public health, Chicago should change the direction of the current of the Chicago River. He was an itinerant professor and then a resident professor in the first medical school in Chicago. He was a great teacher whose students became skillful practitioners and contributed greatly to Dr. Evans' program of making Chicago healthful. In the early days Chicago was twice afflicted with a plague of Asiatic cholera. Dr. Evans made this disease his special object of research. In time he became convinced that it was a communicable disease and that its elimination could be secured by rigid quarantine laws. The commercial and the transportation interests opposed every suggestion of any interference with travel, but Dr. Evans waged a campaign that resulted in the passing of local and national quarantine regulations. These laws eliminated cholera from Chicago, and reduced greatly the spread of other contagious diseases. Besides contributing to Chicago's health, Dr. Evans did much to make Chicago a center of health agencies. Chicago has four grade-A medical schools, eighty hospitals, and is the national headquarters for such organizations as the American Medical Association, the College of Surgeons and Physicians, and the Council on Medical Education and Hospitals. It is not without justice that Chicago is sometimes spoken of as the medical center of America.

To induce highly desirable families to come to Chicago and to remain there Dr. Evans believed that the strengthening of the schools was the most pressing requisite. There existed no organized public school system, no superintendent of public instruction, no high school, and no university. What Dr. Evans did to provide for each of these needs is described in the next chapter. Without his pioneering efforts Chicago could scarcely have become the second—if not the first—educational center in America.

Dr. Evans regarded the churches as second only to the schools in their importance in building a city. In a later chapter the facts will be cited as to the effective support he gave to churches and to the Methodist Church in particular. His foundation work was one of the factors that made it seem appropriate and wise for several of the Boards of the Methodist Church to be established in Chicago, and thus to make Chicago an important headquarters, and possibly the most important headquarters, of Methodism.

As a city builder Dr. Evans attained his greatest success in Evanston. He is credited with having induced the trustees of Northwestern University to purchase several hundred acres of land on Lake Michigan, twelve miles north of Chicago. In fact Mr. Orrington Lunt gives him all the credit for this purchase. This land was surveyed and laid out as the site for Northwestern University and as a suburban community. By action of the Board of Trustees of the University, the new site for the University and for the suburban community was named Evanston.

Of the support given by Dr. Evans individually or through his fellow trustees in building Evanston as an educational center and as a community of homes, the following four unique contributions should be particularly mentioned:

1. *Helpful Restrictions*: The State of Illinois was induced to pass laws prohibiting the sale of intoxicating liquors within four miles of the university campus. By Trustee action industries were not permitted to purchase real estate in Evanston because such ownership might change Evanston from a residential community to an industrial community. For the lots sold by the University the deeds contained the restriction that the land would revert to the University if the owner permitted "intoxicating drink to be manufactured, sold, or given away upon the premise," or permitted "any gambling to be carried on," or permitted thereon "any house or other place of lewd or immoral practices."

2. *Sites Provided*: The University made donations to make Evanston a better community of homes. Included in these donations are sites to twelve churches, two public schools, five private schools, four railroad right of ways, four parks, three public administrative building sites; also many special streets and alleys.

3. *The Utilization of the Lake Front*: The University preserved and protected the Lake front. Before 1853 no university had been located on the shore of a large body of water—ocean, gulf, bay, sea, or great lake. The University was unwilling to sell any large amount of its lake shore holdings to individuals, but retained three quarters of a mile of this frontage for a campus, and donated a sizable frontage to the City. The water-fronts in most cities of the world are occupied by railroads, coal yards, mills, slaughter houses, or other industrial or commercial structures detrimental to a residential suburb. By compelling the railroads to remain away from the lake the University saved the lake shore for Evanston and for the entire residential district from Chicago to Lake Bluff.

4. *Tangible and Intangible Contributions*: The greatest single achievement of Dr. Evans in city building was the support given to Evanston by locating Northwestern University in that prospective suburban community. This support is most intangible, and frequently is not recognized. A few years ago the Evanston Historical Society published a pamphlet in which are described many of the services of the University to the City. After describing these services, the author of the pamphlet states:

> It is easy to see from the foregoing that the University not only originated the village and town, but determined the type of town, the character and

occupation of the people who were to make up that town. Had it not been for the University, Evanston in the natural course of Chicago's growth would some day have existed. Certainly not for twenty-five years, and maybe not for fifty. Its population would have been made up of those forced out of Chicago in search of cheaper living conditions and would have differed greatly from the center of culture, of idealism, with a physical equipment quite in harmony with the environment.

Because of the concentration of specialists, due largely to the University, perhaps no community of its size in America had more leaders in the various governmental departments during the war period. From Evanston came Dawes as Director of Budgets and later Vice President, Dean Wigmore in the Legal Department, Dean Hayford in Aviation, the Head of the Department of Psychology in Personnel, an imposing and important group in the Medical Corps —in fact, all phases and all activities were largely and importantly represented from Evanston's citizenship.

The intangible influence of the University on the City of Evanston is reflected in the comparatively superior quality of citizens who have been attracted to Evanston. In proof of this is the following evidence: Chicago has three major suburbs all of approximately the same size, namely, Evanston, Oak Park, and Cicero. In the current issue of *Who's Who in America* there are listed 223 citizens of Evanston, 38 of Oak Park, and but one of Cicero. Of the citizens of Evanston listed in *Who's Who* 148 are not officially connected with Northwestern University.

What the University means financially to the city is reflected in a recent report of the University Business Office showing that this office had conducted business through the Evanston banks during the last twelve months to the extent of $13,000,000. This does not, of course, include the several millions of dollars spent annually by students and faculty in the Evanston stores and services.

The efforts of Dr. Evans as a city builder in connection with Oreopolis are described in the preceding chapter. It is sufficient to state here that Dr. Evans expected to build Oreopolis to occupy a position on the Great Western Plains comparable to the position that Chicago and Evanston occupy on the Great Lakes.

As a city builder Governor Evans made more diverse types of contributions to Denver than to any other city. How in the interest of Denver he built railroads, founded institutions of higher learning, and supported churches, is stated elsewhere in this sketch. Suffice it here to report on certain other contributions not elsewhere mentioned in this sketch and contributions made only in Denver. In an attempt to increase the natural resources of Colorado he conducted such experiments as the following:

1) He experimented in mining various metals and in smelting by different methods.
2) He invented a plough designed to turn up the subsoil before the term "dry farming" was known.

3) He imported a herd of high grade cattle and secured a large mountain acreage in an endeavor to demonstrate that cattle could be successfully raised in the mountain valleys of the state.

4) He experimented in the cultivation of grapes.

5) He induced the federal government to conduct geological surveys of the mineral lands to aid the people of Colorado to a more scientific development of all kinds of mineral resources.

6) With a view of stimulating search for hidden wealth, he induced the federal government to enact a law giving the property in fee to the discoverers of minerals, under adequate restrictions.

By his political influence he brought to Denver such benefits as the following:

1) Against much opposition he made Denver the permanent capitol city of Colorado.

2) He induced the federal government to deepen the channel into Galveston, then by the extension of his Denver and New Orleans Railroad to Galveston he made Denver a port of entry for imports and exports.

In 1894 Dr. Evans made a final appeal to the city of Denver in the interest of a comprehensive park system connected with encircling parkways and boulevards. His words are self-explanatory:

History is repeating itself in the lifetime of one individual. I was active in starting many of the important enterprises of Chicago for nearly twenty years. President Lincoln then, by appointing me Governor, sent me thirty-two years ago to Pikes Peak, the Territory of Colorado. I found Denver a shanty town of twelve or fifteen hundred inhabitants. I have since then labored faithfully to build up the city, and develop the wonderful resources of the state. Their development, and the growth of the city, are only partially begun, and we have come to the period of preparing a system of parks. The first step in the operation must be the purchase of land, sufficient for a grand system. It will take long years to improve the parks. Afterward the parks cannot be had without the land, and the longer the purchase is delayed the more the land will cost; and if Denver grows rapidly, as it is sure to do, the land will grow in price in a geometrical ratio, so that the interest on the price will be a mere bagatelle compared with the increase in value of the land. The discussion in the papers, and individual opinions given in the last few days, have carried me back to the more bitter discussion of the question in Chicago—and the similarity of the objections—the taxes—the wild prairies—the inopportune time—are identical.

It is true that there is always a large class in every community that is never ready to incur the expense of public improvements—that is never willing to pay its share, and opposes everything that costs money. But I am confident that the people of Denver do not contain a very large proportion of such.

When these words were spoken Governor Evans had been a resident of Denver for thirty-two years, and yet he was as enthusiastic as a boy in promoting plans for the further development of his home city. His plans of 1894 have been developing during all the intervening years, and even today the visitor to Denver sees the ideals of John Evans becoming a reality.

CHAPTER IV.

John Evans, Educator

JOHN EVANS as a youth made a decision that changed the course of his life. His environment, his training, and the insistent desire of his parents seemed to have foreordained him to be a merchant. He expressed his adverse decision in a letter to his cousin, where he summarized his motive and his conclusion: "Only to think of following a trade for no other purpose than my own pecuniary advantage. It is the imperative voice of the Almighty that we shall do all the good we can." John had at that time (1833) become convinced that "to do all the good we can" he must follow the medical profession. During the next six years (1835-41) he completed the work at a medical school, built up a large and lucrative medical practice, and became known as a great leader in the medical profession.

In 1841 he heard Bishop Matthew Simpson deliver his famous lecture on Education. This lecture caused Dr. Evans to reconsider how "to do all the good we can." His conclusion was that although he could through his own practice of medicine do much to promote human welfare he could multiply his usefulness by helping to prepare many young men and women to enter all the professions and all useful occupations.

In 1845 he was invited to become a member of the faculty of the Rush Medical College in Chicago. This invitation was gladly accepted even though for three years (1845-48) he retained his residence in Indianapolis and "commuted" to Chicago by stagecoach. During these commuting years Dr. Evans carried on his medical administration, practiced medicine, and taught medicine, but all the time he was working on a plan to prepare young men and women for services in addition to the practice of medicine. Before the completion of these first three years of teaching Dr. Evans had formulated a plan for establishing a great Christian university. He discussed the matter with Bishop Matthew Simpson and proposed that the Bishop become the president of the institution. Bishop Simpson was unable to free himself from other responsibilities and so declined the presidency of the projected university.

Dr. Evans did not abandon his plan to found a university but only awaited a more favorable opportunity. This fixed purpose—to found a great university—was expressed in the following words:

> There is no other cause to which you can more profitably lend your influence, your labor and your means, than that of Christian education by aiding in founding a university. We may do good by improving the country, by defending it in a righteous cause, by serving it in the councils of legislation on

the bench or in the forum, but these labors are more
or less transient, and the impress we make is tem-
porary, but when we found an institution to mold
minds and characters for good, that will continue its
operations and accumulate influence from generation
to generation through all coming time, we have done
the very highest and noblest service to our country
and our race, of which we are capable. . . .

During the next two years (1848-50) as a resident of Chicago Dr. Evans became acquainted with
the leading business and professional men of that
optimistic town of 28,000 inhabitants. On May 31,
1850, he and eight of his new Chicago friends assembled to plan for the founding of a great university in or near Chicago. Dr. Evans and four others
were selected as a committee to draft a charter for
the University. As soon as the charter was author-
ized by the state legislature in the spring of 1851
Dr. Evans was elected President of the Board. He
was reelected to this office annually thereafter until
1894.

Dr. Evans, together with his fellow trustees,
planned to create a university as good as the best
in New England, and the greatest in all the states
carved out of the Northwest Territory, and therefore a university that might appropriately be called
The Northwestern University. The founders were
Methodists and sought the assistance of the Methodist Conference of five of the Northwest Territory
states and of Iowa in making Northwestern the

leading university affiliated with the Methodist Church. But the university was non-sectarian from the beginning.

Dr. Evans' program of education gave special emphasis to all aspects of education of university grade. However, he was greatly interested also in primary and in secondary education. Furthermore, he recognized the fact that the success of Northwestern University would to a degree be dependent upon the securing of many, and of well-trained, students from the Chicago public school system. His investigation of the status of schools in Chicago revealed to him a most unsatisfactory situation. The elementary schools were not organized into a school system, there was no superintendent of schools, there was no public high school, and the school lands were not being administered wisely. Accordingly, he became a candidate for membership on the Chicago Board of Aldermen on a school-betterment platform and was elected in 1853. He was made chairman of the School Committee and introduced an ordinance requiring the organization of a public school system, the appointment of a superintendent, and the creation of a public high school. He also succeeded in restoring and preserving part of the school lands for the support of public instruction.

The school lands originally consisted of the tract extending from Madison to Twelfth Streets, and from State almost to Halsted. The following is his description of an instance of his success in regaining some of the school land:

> They were selling all their school lands and school property, and I put a stop to that. For instance, there were eighty acres in one block that they had sold, and the purchaser had made default, and the land reverted back. They wanted to resell it, and I would not allow it.

The citizens of Chicago appreciated this service, as indicated by the following quotation from the *Chicago Republic* of September 14, 1866:

> 'Tis a noteworthy circumstance that the school fund of the city as well as of the Northwestern University is incalculably indebted to the sagacity of Governor Evans.
>
> Coming into the City Council while the school lands were being recklessly squandered, and being made chairman of the school committee, he succeeded in arresting the city fathers in their "mad career" and prevailed upon them by the report of his committee to lease rather than sell their school land, saying, "Gentlemen, stop selling until Chicago stops growing." From that day we believe there has been no school property sold; but if the selling had never begun, the Chicago funds would now be worth more like twelve million than a million and a half in value.

Soon after he became President of the Board of Trustees of Northwestern University Dr. Evans took a leading part in the securing of a site or sites for the University. In 1851 he purchased in his name sixteen lots at the corner of what is now Jackson and LaSalle Streets for $8,000. By 1854 the value of this site had enhanced greatly but the trustees desired these lots for the site for their proposed preparatory school. He thereupon sold the lots to the University for $8,000, and was a chief contributor also to the payment fund.

In 1853 Dr. Evans and Orrington Lunt together with two other trustees were appointed as a committee to select a site for the University. Mr. Lunt first discovered the wooded 379-acre tract on the shore of Lake Michigan, twelve miles north of Chicago. However, Dr. Evans took the initiative in securing this tract for the University.

From 1851 to 1894 Dr. Evans served not merely as the President of the Board of Trustees of Northwestern University; in reality for that period he was the University's chief educational leader and financial benefactor.

The original plan of the founders of Northwestern was to establish an undergraduate and a graduate college of liberal arts, and also to establish related schools of law, medicine, and theology. Of these three professional schools theology was the first to receive consideration. In 1854 Dr. Evans and four others agreed to erect a building and to provide for a number of years a fund for the support of Garrett Biblical Institute. A site for Garrett was made available on the Northwestern campus. Garrett was founded and continued as an independent institution but affiliated with Northwestern.

As early as 1845 Dr. Evans had become convinced that Chicago would ultimately become the metropolis of the states carved out of the Northwest territory. His endeavors to make Northwestern University an institution that would serve this geographical area had by 1859 been sufficiently successful to be regarded by him as most gratifying and encouraging. At this time (1859) as stated in the previous chapter Dr. Evans became convinced that in the near future a railroad would be built from Chicago to the Rockies; that this road would probably cross the Missouri river at the confluence of this and the Platte River; that a great metropolis would probably arise at this place; and that a university established there in advance would exercise a beneficial influence on the development of all these western plains. He acquired a large tract of land for the site of the city, secured a charter for a university, and obtained for it the sponsorship of the Methodist conferences. He was repeating the program followed in the creation of Northwestern University and the village of Evanston, except that all was to be on the scale of a Chicago rather than of an Evanston. This city, located on the border between Iowa and Nebraska, he named Oreopolis, the Greek equivalent of the English words, *border city*. He gave to the University also the name of Oreopolis University.

The following quotation is from a letter of

Dr. Evans to his wife and indicates that his chief interest in Oreopolis was in the proposed university:

> We had a spirited contest before the conference for its adoption of our institution at Oreopolis. Nebraska City contended for the University with great energy, but we came off triumphant. The Conference adopted all of our institutions by an almost unanimous vote. Oreopolis is now well established and well advertised as the contest has given us a very general notoriety. Building is going on very rapidly. The hotel is not finished but will go on rapidly from this time. Our own ferry-boat arrived today and will do well.

The anticipated railroad ultimately crossed the Missouri not at Oreopolis but farther north where Omaha and Council Bluffs now stand. As a result the plans for the university and for the city of Oreopolis were abandoned.

When Dr. Evans was made Governor of the territory of Colorado in 1862 he assumed responsibility for the educational needs of that territory. The immigrants to Colorado were frequently families in which the children had been taken from the schools of the East, and adequate schools were not available in the sparsely settled districts, and not even in Denver, a town of 3,000 inhabitants. In 1863 Governor Evans requested the cooperation of the Colorado Conference of the Methodist Church in establishing an institution of higher learning to be called the Colorado Seminary. He was unable to secure substantial financial cooperation in the early years for the Seminary, the first head of the school died, debts were incurred with interest rate 3 per cent monthly, and finally instruction was discontinued, and the executive and legislative offices of the Territory were installed in the Seminary buildings.

The number of academy and of college students in Colorado was small, but each of the religious denominations was attempting to retain or to establish some type of higher learning. In the interests of the students of Colorado, Governor Evans proposed that the official bodies of the churches represented in Colorado should merge their efforts into making one worthwhile institution to be called the Union Evangelical University. He appeared in person before the official boards of the Methodist, Presbyterian, Episcopal, and Baptist Churches. He presented the plan and took part in deliberations. He was quite sure that each demonination would agree to the program; so he appeared before the Denver Board of Trade to secure the cooperation of the citizenry of Denver as additional support. In the address which he delivered to the Board of Trade the following statement was made:

> A well-founded university lives as long as the country in which it is founded lives. It lives for ages. Its influence runs through all time . . . . Why, there is nothing in all a man's lifetime that he can do that will be so permanent in its beneficial results as founding an institution of learning that will live on, and

> work, year after year, age after age, after he is laid
> in the grave.

Unfortunately, certain denominations failed to cooperate, and the program for the Union Evangelical University was dropped in 1874.

From 1867 to 1879 the Colorado Seminary remained practically inactive except for his efforts to keep it alive and create interest in the cause of higher learning. The status of the institution had sunk so low that the other trustees asked Governor Evans to pay its debts and hold its property until the enterprise could be revived. By 1879 the high schools in Denver were making provision for secondary education, and the term "Seminary" had become an uninspiring name for an institution of higher learning. Furthermore, the citizens of Denver desired an institution not so exclusively dependent upon the Methodist Church but one that had more the characteristics of a municipal university. It was proposed that this new institution should be called the University of Denver. Governor Evans also agreed to donate land for the proposed university and agreed to match dollar for dollar all donations made to create and endow it.

Governor Evans served as President of the Board of Trustees of the Colorado Seminary from 1864 to 1879 and of the University of Denver and Colorado Seminary from 1879 to 1897. He was succeeded in the Presidency of the Board by his son,

William G. Evans, who in turn was succeeded by his son, John Evans, who is still the Chairman of the Board of Trustees.

In a period of thirty-four years Dr. Evans attempted to found four new universities and to bring about two mergers. In each of these six endeavors he was not only the directing genius but he was in every case the sole or the chief financial contributor. Of all his many activities those connected with universities brought to him his greatest satisfaction. All friends of Northwestern are pleased to know that his chief delight was in Northwestern, and that many of his largest benefactions were given to this institution.

CHAPTER V.

John Evans, Religious Leader

JOHN EVANS was born of Quaker parents and even as a youth manifested strong religious convictions. He possessed a firm faith in the supremacy of spiritual values and in the ultimate triumph of the right. He avoided every tendency to seek primarily his pecuniary advantage but was motivated by a desire to serve God and his fellow men.

While practicing medicine in Attica Dr. Evans became impressed with the practical idealism of Bishop Simpson and certain other members of the Methodist Church. Accordingly, Dr. Evans joined the little local Methodist Church in Attica, where he immediately exerted a dominating influence.

His support of the Church was significant not only in Attica but also in Indianapolis, Chicago, Evanston, and Denver. As outstanding instances of his financial contributions to Methodist churches the following should be cited: the building of the Methodist Church block in Chicago; the providing of one-fifth of the support of Garrett Biblical Institute in Evanston for a number of years; the sole or the principal financial contributions in Denver to the First Methodist Church and parsonage, to the Evans Mission Sunday School and the Evans

Memorial Chapel, to the Grace Methodist Church, and to the First German Methodist Church; generous donations in Denver to the North Denver and Asbury Methodist Church, and to Christ Methodist Church. He gave financial support also to the churches of other Protestant denominations, and to various Catholic institutions. For many years he contributed not less than $100 to every church of any denomination started in Colorado. As Carnegie built libraries, and as Rosenwald built school houses, Evans built churches.

Dr. Evans was an administrative and a spiritual leader in the Methodist Church even to a greater extent than he was a financial leader.

Until 1868 the authority of the Methodist Church was vested in the General Conference, in which the membership was restricted to bishops and ministers. The theory was that laymen were not qualified to pass judgment on theological questions. Dr. Evans with others called a conference in Chicago to draft a request, which the General Conference granted, that laymen be admitted to membership and that the Conference be democratized.

As soon as laymen were admitted to membership and to active participation in the General Conference of the Methodist Church Dr. Evans was elected as a lay member and his re-election to membership seems to have been continuous till his declining years. The list of the important committees of the Conference on which he served includes the following: Episcopacy, Itinerancy, Book Concern, Education, Church Extension, State of the Church, Freeman's Aid and Southern Work, Lay Representation, Sunday Schools and Tracts, Temperance and Prohibition of the Liquor Traffic. He is credited with having a large part in the establishing of the Methodist Book Concern and was one of the founders and supporters of the *Northwestern Christian Advocate*.

In his support of churches, in his administration of ecclesiastical procedures, and in his leadership in applied Christianity, Dr. Evans ranks as one of the greatest religious leaders among laymen of his generation.

For Dr. Evans religion had to do not only with man's relationship with God, but also with man's relationship with men. Accordingly, besides being interested in ecclesiastical Christianity he was interested in applied Christianity—in worshipping God by righting human wrongs. The first great human wrong that Dr. Evans tried to remove was that of the neglect and abuse of the insane, the blind, and the deaf. His devotion to these unfortunate fellow creatures brought about speedy relief in Indiana and hastened the movement in several other states.

The grandfather of John Evans was a slave holder in North Carolina; but he married a Quakeress who convinced him that slavery was wrong. He freed his slaves and left the state. John was raised in an anti-slavery home but was inclined to regard slavery as more or less a necessary evil. However, while still a practicing physician in Attica he had occasion to make an extensive trip through the slave states extending as far south as New Orleans. As a result of his personal observations he became a staunch enemy of slavery and an active propagandist for abolition. If not actually a "conductor" on the "underground railway," he was known to have assisted runaway slaves in their attempts to reach Canada. Through his abolitionist efforts he formed a close friendship with Abraham Lincoln and with many of the national leaders in the restriction or abolition of slavery. In the foundation of the Republican Party, Governor Evans represented the anti-slavery interests, and as the war governor of Colorado, by his strenuous efforts to raise troops for the Union Army he contributed much to the success of the war which freed the slaves.

Dr. Evans regarded the traditional treatment of women as an injustice second only to our treatment of the colored race. He contended that women should not be discriminated against in such institutions, activities, and relationships as schools, professions, and the right to vote and hold public office. His support of women's rights resulted in advancing women wherever he had authority. Thus, Northwestern University, of which he was president of the board of trustees, was one of the first institutions in America to admit women in all its schools on an equality with men. Thus, the Rush faculty, of which he was an influential member, was one of the first medical faculties in America to grant a medical degree to a woman. Thus, at a time when no state or territory gave women the right to vote, he tried to get the franchise for women in Colorado, and Colorado was the second state in the Union to grant suffrage to women. Thus, Dr. Evans supported and worked with Susan B. Anthony and others of those who eventually secured the amendment to our national constitution which removed the injustice of sex discrimination in the right to vote.

The mother of John Evans was a prohibitionist and regarded the liquor traffic as one of the greatest of all human wrongs. To prevent the sale of "the poisonous concoctions of the Evil One" in Waynesville, she employed tactics which, though not as spectacular as Carrie Nation's, were quite as effective. John Evans likewise regarded the liquor traffic as one of our great human wrongs, and he did what he could to reduce it. He was merely one among the millions of workers for prohibition, but credit should be given him for the fact that liquor has never been sold legally in Evanston—the city that bears his name. He must receive some credit also for the fact that the greatest prohibition leader of all times—Frances Willard—was a product of Evanston and one of his close personal friends.

In his support of churches, in his administration of ecclesiastical procedures, and in his leadership in applied Christianity, Dr. Evans ranks as one of the greatest religious leaders among laymen of his generation.

CHAPTER VI.

John Evans, Political Leader

A POLITICAL leader is one who is capable of selecting cooperative associates and of welding them into an effective unit.

The success of John Evans in selecting his co-workers is illustrated by his selection of Dr. N. S. Davis for medicine, Bishop Matthew Simpson for religion, Orrington Lunt for educational administration, Dorothea Lynde Dix for care of the insane, Frances Willard for prohibition, Abraham Lincoln for anti-slavery. In many of his cooperative efforts he confined himself to a minor role while the major role was played by a friend.

The group or party in which John Evans was a leader consisted sometimes of but two or a few members, sometimes of a score or a hundred, and in at least three instances it included the majority of the voting members in the Whig, the Democratic, or the Republican party in a small or a large geographical political area. In all his activities he merged himself so completely in the group of which he was a member that it is impossible to give credit to individuals. However, he was an inspiring personality and exercised a directing influence in every group or party of which he was a member. He frequently spent many hours in planning for important ventures, but when it came to the execution of the plan he depended upon group action.

A political leader is one who thinks constructively in terms of local, state, and national welfare, and who is willing to seek election or to accept appointment to office in one or all of these geographical political divisions.

John Evans was the intellectual leader in *local* problems having to do with health, religion, and education in Attica, Chicago, Evanston, and Denver. He was elected alderman in Chicago, and as a member of the Council served on the committees on schools, wharves, public grounds, and wharfing privileges. He was appointed to offices having to do with various humanitarian problems in the other communities where he made his home.

He thought constructively also on such *state* problems as the care of the insane in Indiana, the support of private institutions of higher learning in Illinois, and the problem of transportation in Colorado. He accepted the position of Commissioner and then later of Superintendent of the State Hospital for the Insane in Indiana, and filled many state positions of trust and of importance in Colorado.

He demonstrated that he was a constructive thinker on such *national* questions as slavery, women's rights, prohibition, national quarantine, and governmental supervision of business. He was appointed by Abraham Lincoln as the war Governor of the Colorado Territory. Under his governorship Colorado furnished in relation to her population a greater ratio of soldiers to the Union Army than any other state or territory. He was elected the first Senator of the United States from Colorado (the statehood was denied by veto of President Andrew Johnson).

A political leader in America is one who is a leader in a political party or parties.

As a youth John Evans seemed to take little interest in political parties, but much interest in public issues. He was opposed to slavery, and probably classified himself as a Whig. As a young practicing physician in Attica, Fountain County, Indiana, he made a political issue of human rights, but in this movement the Whig party took but little interest. Accordingly, Dr. Evans turned for assistance to the Democratic party. By his influence with the Quakers and the Methodists he became a state leader of the Democratic party in the state of Indiana. The following is a quotation from an historian of that period:

The lack of interest displayed by Governor Bigger in the movement for an insane hospital was one of the deciding factors in his defeat for re-election in 1843. The Democrats at that time came out on a platform of human rights and individual liberty, and this platform contained a plank declaring it the duty of the state to care for the unfortunate and feeble. The Methodists had become a power in the state, and, as the ranks of this church had been largely recruited from the Society of Friends, with whom Dr. Evans was on the best of terms, the Fountain County junta was able to wield an influence extending far beyond the natural confines of the district. President Simpson of Indiana Asbury, who had become a political power, also threw his great influence in the scales to help his friends in Attica. They pleaded for human rights, individual liberty, private initiative; that it was more the duty of the state to care for the unfortunate, the feeble, educate the children, and foster individual development than to concern itself entirely with aiding bankers, manufacturers and transportation companies. The coalition of Methodists and Democrats drove the Whig party from power after eighteen successive years. Governor James Whitcomb and other state officials were deeply indebted to Dr. Evans for the part that he had played, and when he appeared before them in behalf of the insane hospital the handicap under which he had labored was gone.

That John Evans was a leader in the Republican party, even in the early days of that party, is demonstrated by the following historical facts:

An informal group of anti-slavery citizens in Ripon, Wisconsin, adopted the term "Republican Party" on July 6, 1854.

A group of editors met in Bloomington, Illinois, and adopted the slogan "Freedom is national but slavery is local," on February 22, 1856. They also issued a call for a state convention of editors.

This state convention of editors convened in Bloomington, Illinois, May 29, 1856. The Chicago representative, William B. Ogden, could not be present, and his place was taken by Dr. Evans, the only man to attend not an active editor. He took a prominent part in the organization, and was considered for nomination as candidate for Congress on the Republican ticket the following fall. Previous to the election he was asked for an expression of his view on slavery, this inquiry coming in the form of a questionnaire from the Hon. W. B. Plato of Geneva. The letter which framed the reply, issued four years before the Republican party had elected Lincoln president, was a clear-cut political statement upon a question which politicians were then endeavoring to avoid by generalizations:

Chicago, September 4th, 1856.

Your favor of the 23 ult. was duly received upon my arrival at home on the 28th, and should have had a prompt reply, but my health would not justify the effort until now. I thank you for information that my letter of acceptance is not sufficiently explicit on the subject of slavery, and shall cheerfully answer your several questions. But before proceeding I will state the general proposition: that I believe it to be the duty of the general government in all cases where it has the authority over the subject, to exercise its positive influence in favor of freedom and against slavery. A position of neutrality on the subject of liberty by a government founded as ours was for the promotion and enjoyment of freedom; and established at the expense of the treasure and blood of the patriots of the Revolution, would be a spectacle of degeneracy too humiliating to be contemplated with complacency, or tolerated by an enlightened and virtuous people. You ask,

Ques. 1st: Do you believe Congress has the Constitutional power to prohibit slavery in the territories of the United States and if elected, will you endeavor to procure such prohibition?

Ans.: Inasmuch as the Constitution expressly gives Congress the power to "make all needful rules and regulations respecting the territory, or other property belonging to the United States"—and since Congress has always heretofore exercised the authority of enacting laws for the regulations and government of the people who might settle in the territories, I do not see how it can be regarded as unconstitutional for it to prohibit any great moral, social and political evil from being introduced into them, all of which slavery is admitted to be by every right-thinking person in the country, whether an inhabitant of the North or South.

Ques. 2nd: Do you believe Congress has power to abolish slavery in the District of Columbia; and, if elected, will you use your best endeavors to procure such prohibition?

Answer: With the clear and unequivocal declaration in the Constitution: "Congress shall have power to exercise exclusive legislation in all cases, whatsoever, over such district (not exceeding ten miles square), as may by cession of particular states, and acceptance of Congress become the seat of government of the United States," I do not see how anyone can entertain a doubt in reference to Congress having the power: and as a majority of the voters of the district have petitioned for it, I should, if elected, use my best endeavors to remove from our nation that blackest spot upon her fair name, slavery in the national capitol.

Ques. 3rd: Are you in favor of admitting more slave states into the Union; and how would you vote upon the application of any new state for admission with a Constitution that recognizes the institution of slavery?

Answer: I am not in favor of the admission of any more slave states; and I should vote against such application.

Ques. 4th: Are you in favor of a repeal or amendment of the fugitive slave law of 1850; or do you regard it as a just and constitutional law of the land?

Answer: I regard the law which, either directly or indirectly, denies any person whatsoever, in times of peace and safety, the benefit of those constitutionally guaranteed safeguards to liberty, the writ of habeas corpus, and the right of trial by jury, as dangerous and unjust; and therefore should be in favor of the amendment of said law so as to fully secure those rights. And, in case such amendment cannot be made, rather than retain the law in its present form, I should vote for its entire repeal.

Hoping my answers may prove satisfactory to yourself and the people of this district generally, I grant the permission you ask to lay them before the public, and with sentiments of great respect, remain very truly,

Your obedient servant,
JOHN EVANS

Governor John Evans was a political leader—a very great political leader—when adjudged according to each of the three searching standards here applied.

Conclusion

In the foreword the statement was made that John Evans was to be presented as a physician, as a railroad builder, as a city builder, as an educator, as a religious leader, and as a political leader. In each of the six chapters an attempt has been made to present concrete verifiable facts descriptive of the achievements of John Evans in one of these particular fields. In each field his contributions were extraordinary.

The writer believes that equally laudatory chapters could be truthfully written concerning John Evans as a man, as a husband, as a father, as a neighbor, as a citizen, and as a friend.